Christopher Goldston

FANTASTIC FINGERS

BOOK 2

Notes from the Publisher

Composers in Focus is a series of original piano collections celebrating the creative artistry of contemporary composers. It is through the work of these composers that the piano teaching repertoire is enlarged and enhanced.

It is my hope that students, teachers, and all others who experience this music will be enriched and inspired.

Frank J Hackinson

Frank J. Hackinson, Publisher

Notes from the Composer

Fantastic Fingers is a series of original piano solos that feel good to play and fall easily under the fingers. *Book 2* consists of elementary solos mainly centered in C, G, and Middle C positions. The accessible patterns in these pieces make them both easy to learn and memorize.

I wish to thank Frank Hackinson for his support of my musical endeavors. With his enthusiastic help, I have created the second collection in this series for The FJH Music Company Inc. Have fun exploring the variety of sounds and styles inside this collection. I'm sure you will find them as pleasing to the ear as they are fun to play!

Christopher Goldston

Christopher Goldston

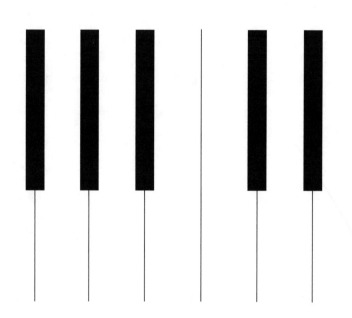

Contents

Cool Cat Strut

Feel the rhythmic strut as you play this piece.
You may wish to tap the beats first.

Christopher Goldston

With a jazzy beat

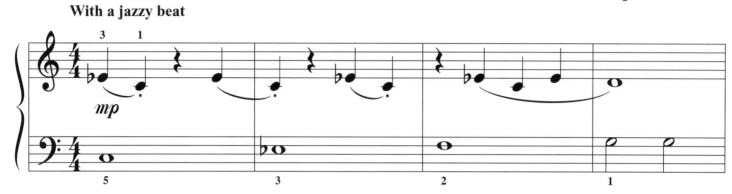

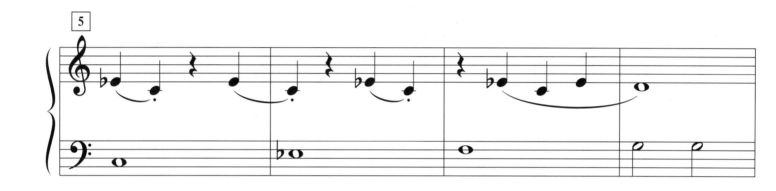

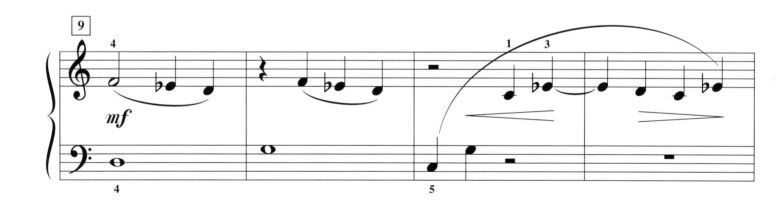

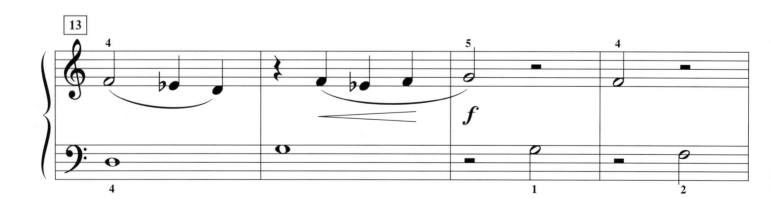

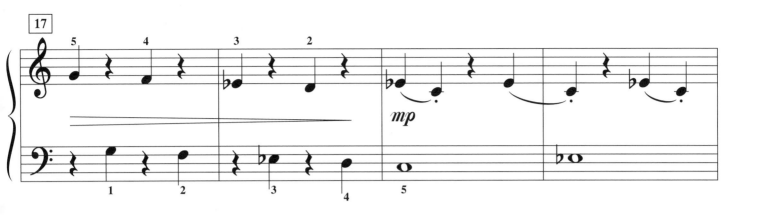

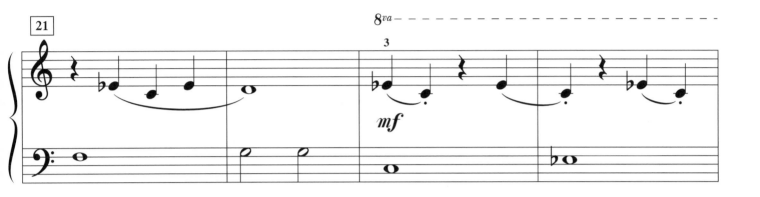

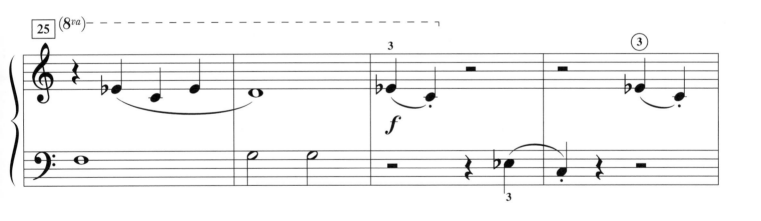

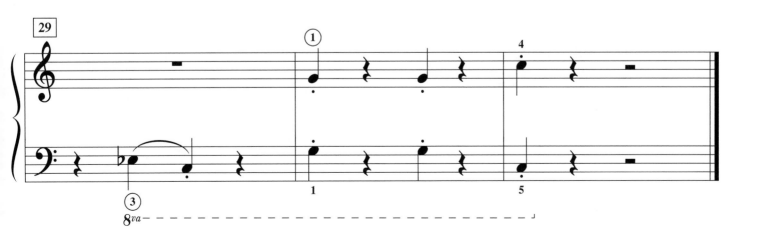

Brave Hawk

Play this piece with great dignity to celebrate
the pride of the Native American people.

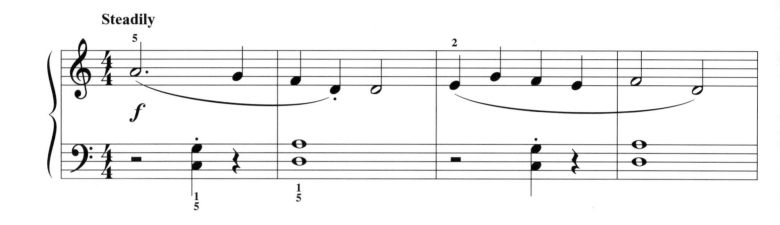

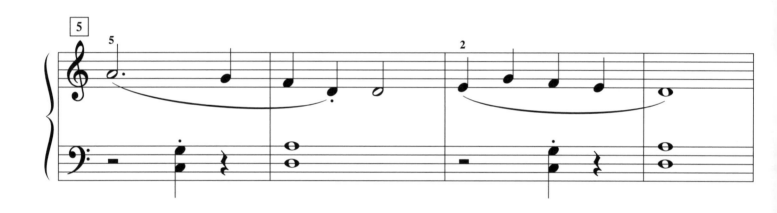

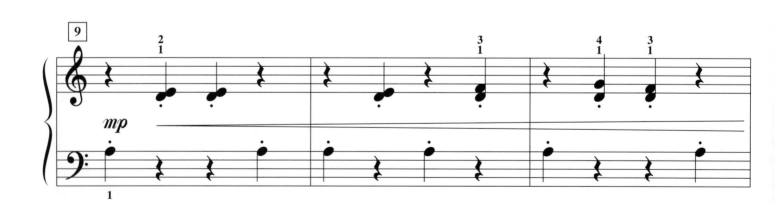

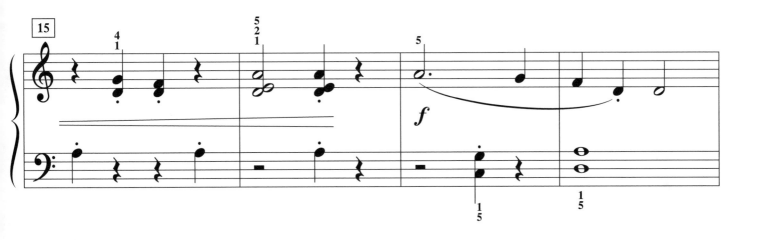

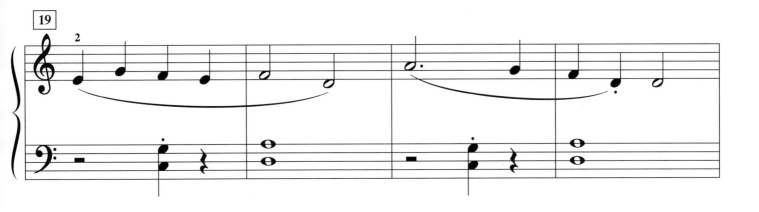

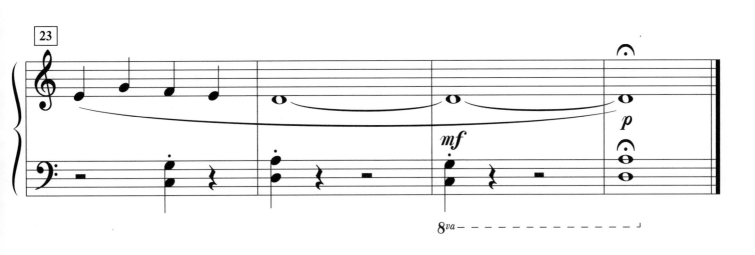

Luck of the Irish

This happy jig should be played with great enthusiasm.

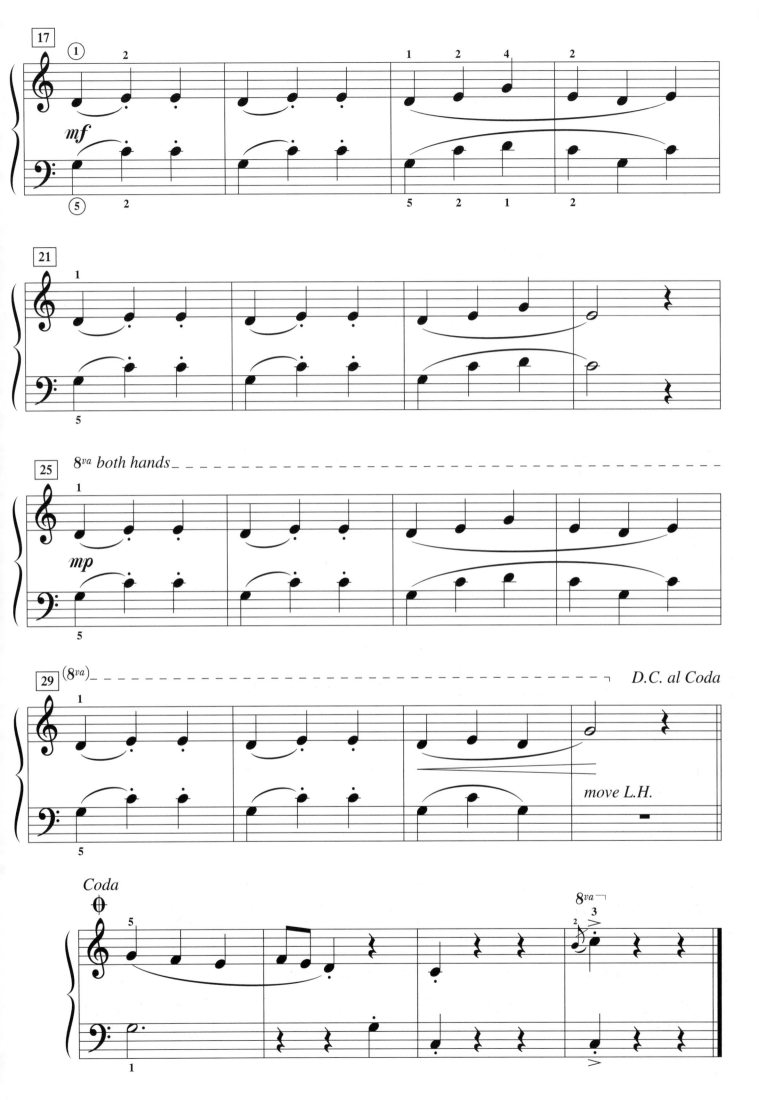

Snake Charmer

Play this melody smoothly, like a snake
slithering its way out of a charmer's basket.

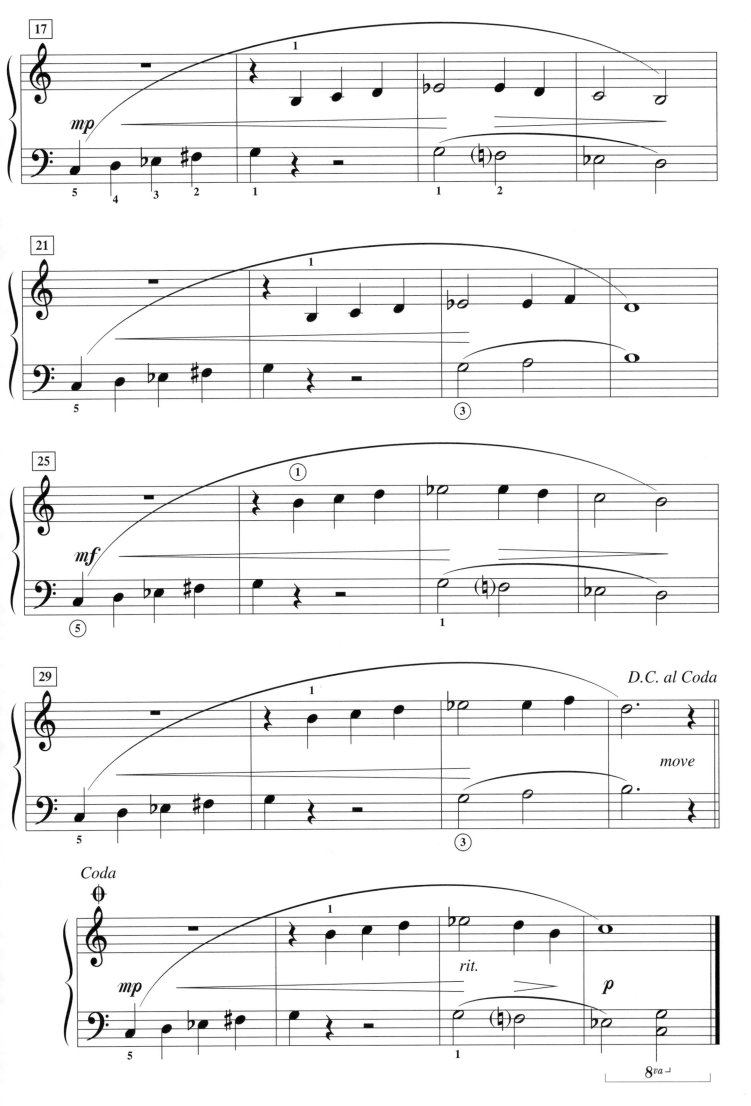

London Chimes

Ring the bells of this melody with confidence and joy!

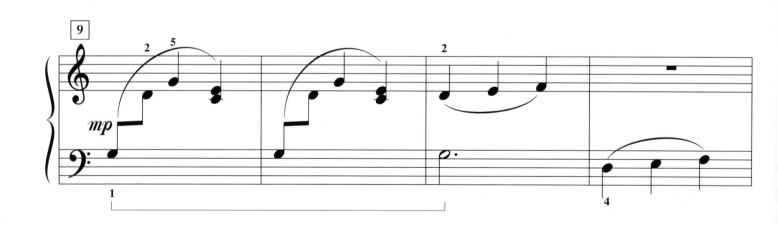

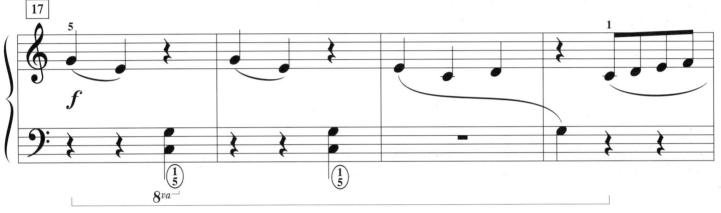

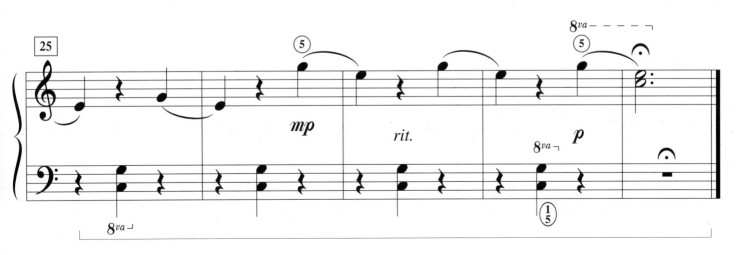

FF1275

Temple Breezes

Imagine the wind blowing gently
as you play this pentatonic melody.

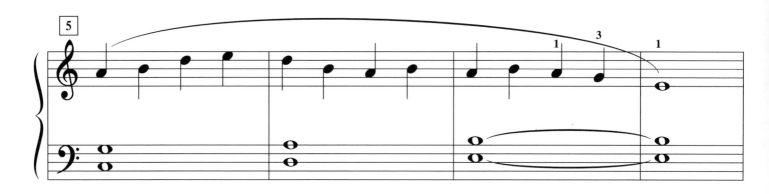

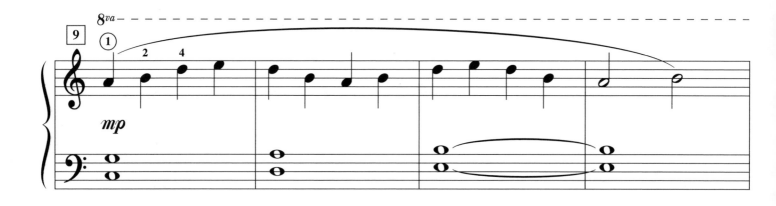

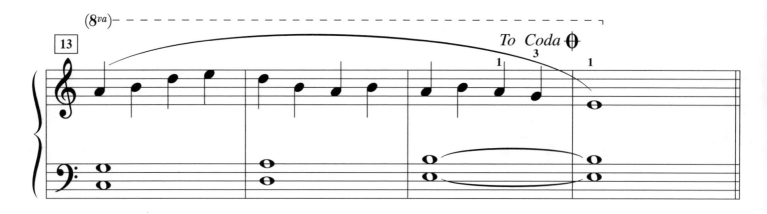

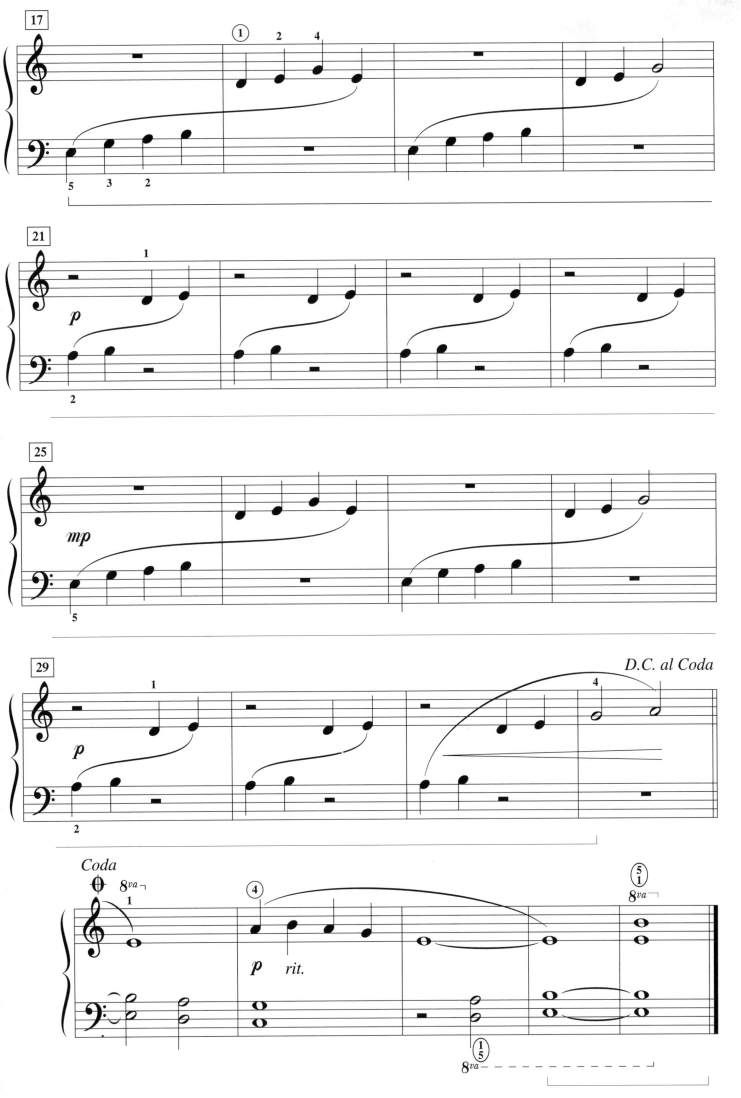

Whirlwind

Don't stop to take a breath. Play as fast
as you can, but keep a steady tempo.

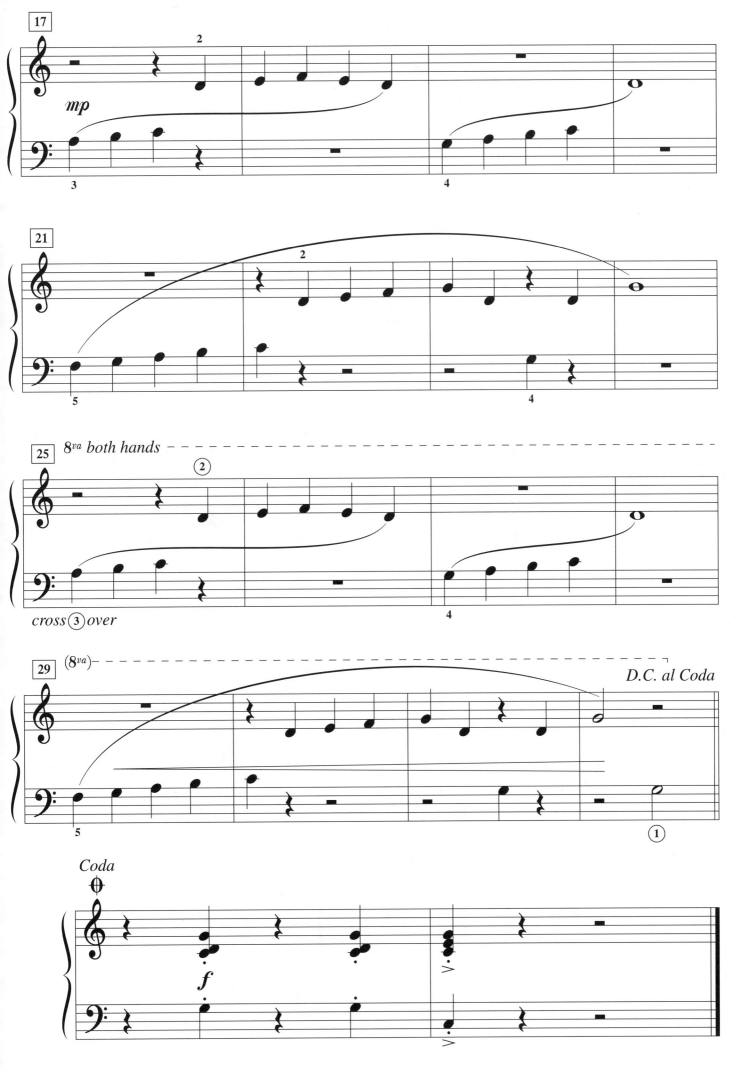

Night Flight

Imagine flying through the night sky
as you play this mysterious piece.

Very quickly

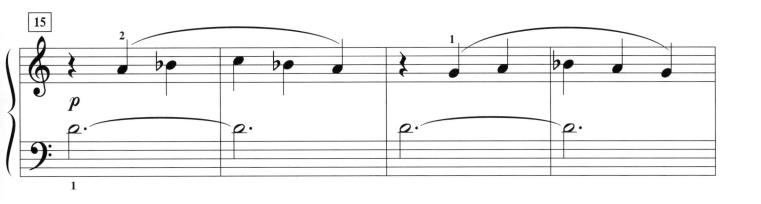

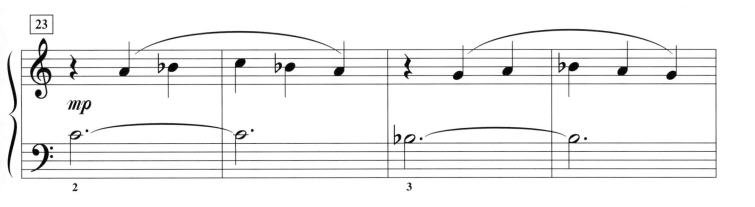

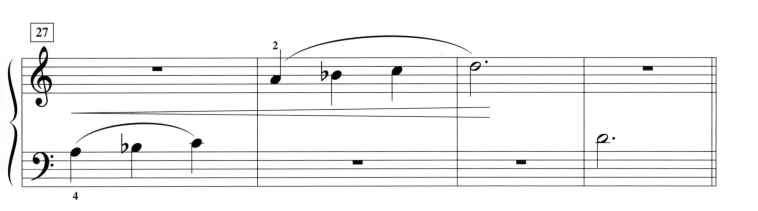

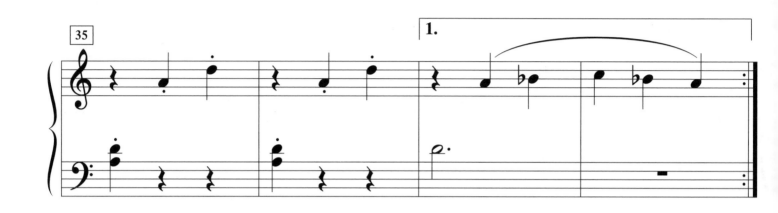

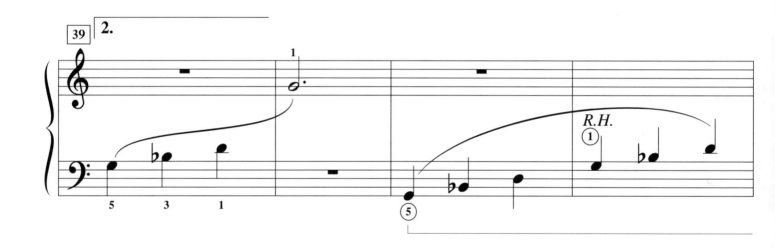

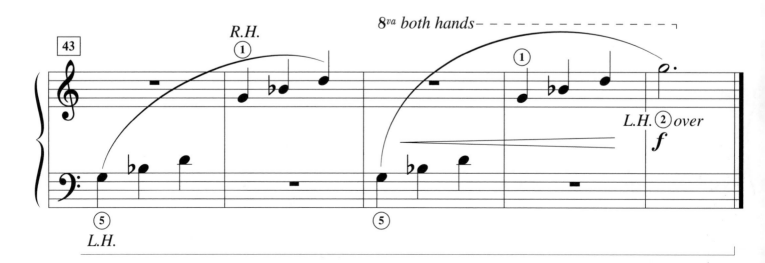